CompTIA Fundamentals FC0-U71 Exam Preparation:

Domain 1 - IT Concepts and Terminology

1.1 – Basics of Computing

Computing involves four primary functions: input, processing, output, and storage. Understanding these basic concepts is essential for anyone interested in technology. Input refers to the data or commands entered into a computer system. Once input is received, processing occurs, where the computer's CPU (Central Processing Unit) manipulates the data to produce meaningful information. Output is the result of this processing, which can be displayed on a screen, printed on paper, or sent to another device. Finally, storage is where data is saved for future use, allowing for retrieval and editing as needed.

Fill in the Blank: Fill in the blank with the correct words.

1. The act of entering data into a computer system is called _.
2. The _ is responsible for processing data within a computer.
3. The result of processed data is known as _.
4. Information saved for future use is stored in the computer's _.
5. A keyboard is an example of an _ device.

Word bank: storage, input, output, input, CPU

Multiple Choice Questions: Choose the correct answer from the choices for each question.

1. What is the primary function of the CPU in a computer?
   A. To store data
   B. To process data
   C. To display information
   D. To input data
2. Which of the following is an example of an output device?
   A. Mouse
   B. Printer
   C. Scanner
   D. Keyboard
3. What type of storage is typically used for long-term data retention?
   A. RAM
   B. Cache
   C. Hard Drive
   D. CPU
4. Which device is primarily used to enter data into a computer?
   A. Monitor
   B. Printer
   C. Keyboard
   D. CPU
5. What happens during the processing stage in computing?
   A. Data is stored
   B. Data is entered
   C. Data is manipulated
   D. Data is displayed

Open Ended Questions: Answer the following questions in complete sentences:

1. Explain the difference between input and output in computing.
2. Describe the role of storage in a computer system.
3. Why is the processing stage critical in the computing process?

Answer Key:

Fill in the Blank:

1. input
2. CPU
3. output
4. storage
5. input

Multiple Choice Questions:

1. B. To process data
2. B. Printer
3. C. Hard Drive
4. C. Keyboard
5. C. Data is manipulated

Open Ended Questions:

1. Input refers to the data or commands entered into a computer system, while output is the information or results produced after the data has been processed.
2. Storage in a computer system is responsible for saving data so it can be retrieved and used later. It ensures that information is not lost and can be accessed when needed.
3. The processing stage is critical because it is where data is manipulated and transformed into meaningful information, allowing users to make decisions or perform tasks based on the processed data.

1.2 - Understanding Notational Systems

Notational systems are used to represent numbers in different bases. The most common systems are binary, hexadecimal, decimal, and octal. Each system has its own base and is used in various computing contexts. The binary system, with a base of 2, uses only the digits 0 and 1. Hexadecimal, with a base of 16, uses digits 0-9 and letters A-F. The decimal system, which we use in everyday life, has a base of 10. Octal is a base 8 system, using digits 0-7. Understanding these systems is crucial for computer science and IT professionals.

Fill in the Blank: Fill in the blank with the correct words.

1. The binary system uses a base of __.
2. In hexadecimal notation, the letter 'A' represents the decimal number __.
3. The decimal system is also known as base __.
4. Octal notation uses digits ranging from _ to _.
5. The number '1011' in binary is equal to __ in decimal.

Word bank: 16, 2, 10, 11, 0, 7

Multiple Choice Questions: Choose the correct answer from the choices for each question.

1. What is the base of the octal system?
   - A) 2
   - B) 8
   - C) 10
   - D) 16
2. Which notational system is primarily used in computing for addressing memory?
   - A) Decimal
   - B) Octal
   - C) Binary
   - D) Hexadecimal
3. How many unique symbols does the hexadecimal system use?
   - A) 8
   - B) 10
   - C) 12
   - D) 16
4. What is the binary equivalent of the decimal number 5?
   - A) 101
   - B) 110
   - C) 111
   - D) 100
5. In octal notation, what does the digit '7' represent in binary?
   - A) 001
   - B) 010
   - C) 111
   - D) 100

Open Ended Questions: Answer the following questions in complete sentences:

1. Explain how you convert a binary number to a decimal number.

2. Describe a scenario where hexadecimal notation might be more beneficial than binary or decimal.

3. Discuss the importance of understanding different notational systems in the field of computer science.

Answer Key:

Fill in the Blank:

1. 2
2. 10
3. 10
4. 0, 7
5. 11

Multiple Choice Questions:

1. B) 8
2. D) Hexadecimal
3. D) 16
4. A) 101
5. C) 111

Open Ended Questions:

1. To convert a binary number to a decimal number, multiply each bit by 2 raised to the power of its position index, starting from the rightmost bit which is at index 0. Sum all the results to get the decimal number.
2. Hexadecimal notation is beneficial in scenarios like digital electronics or computer programming where memory addresses are represented, as it is more compact and easier to read than binary.
3. Understanding different notational systems is crucial in computer science because it helps in data representation, memory addressing, and efficient coding. It allows professionals to work effectively across various computing environments.

1.3 - Understanding Units of Measure

To effectively manage and use computer systems, it's essential to understand different units of measure. This includes storage units like Bits and Bytes, throughput units such as Bits per second, and processing speed measured in Hertz.

Fill in the Blank: Fill in the blank with the correct words.

1. A _ is the smallest unit of data in a computer.
2. One _ is equal to 1,024 Kilobytes.
3. Internet speed is often measured in _ per second.
4. A CPU's speed is typically measured in _.
5. A _ is larger than a Terabyte.

Word bank: Kilobyte, Gigabyte, Bit, Petabyte, Megahertz, Megabits

Multiple Choice Questions: Choose the correct answer from the choices for each question.

1. Which of the following is the largest unit of storage?
   - a) Megabyte
   - b) Gigabyte
   - c) Terabyte
   - d) Petabyte
2. What does Mbps stand for?
   - a) Millions of bytes per second
   - b) Megabits per second
   - c) Megabytes per second
   - d) Microbytes per second
3. How many bytes are in a Kilobyte?
   - a) 100
   - b) 1,024
   - c) 1,000
   - d) 10,000
4. What unit is used to measure the speed of a processor?
   - a) Bits per second
   - b) Hertz
   - c) Bytes
   - d) Pixels
5. What is the unit of measurement for data transfer rate?
   - a) Bytes
   - b) Hertz
   - c) Bits per second
   - d) Inches

Open Ended Questions: Answer the following questions in complete sentences:

1. Explain the difference between a Byte and a Bit.
2. Why is understanding data throughput important for internet services?

3. Describe a scenario where a higher processing speed would be beneficial.

Answer Key:

Fill in the Blank:

1. Bit
2. Megabyte
3. Megabits
4. Megahertz
5. Petabyte

Multiple Choice Questions:

1. d) Petabyte
2. b) Megabits per second
3. b) 1,024
4. b) Hertz
5. c) Bits per second

Open Ended Questions:

1. A Byte is a unit of digital information that consists of 8 Bits. A Bit is the smallest unit of data in a computer and can be either 0 or 1.
2. Understanding data throughput is important for internet services because it determines how fast data can be transferred over the internet, affecting download and upload speeds and overall internet performance.
3. A higher processing speed would be beneficial in scenarios such as gaming or video editing, where fast data processing is required for smooth performance and quick response times.

1.4 - Troubleshooting Methodology

Troubleshooting is a step-by-step approach to solving problems in technology. It involves identifying an issue, creating and testing theories to fix it, and ensuring the solution works effectively. This process is essential for IT professionals to resolve technical issues efficiently.

Fill in the Blank: Fill in the blank with the correct words.

1. The first step in troubleshooting is to _ the problem.
2. After identifying the problem, you should establish a _ of probable cause.
3. You might need to _ the internet or knowledge base for more information.
4. Once a theory is tested, you should establish a plan of action to _ the problem.
5. It's important to _ full system functionality after implementing a solution.

Word bank: verify, resolve, theory, research, identify

Multiple Choice Questions: Choose the correct answer from the choices for each question.

1. What is the first step in the troubleshooting methodology?
   - a) Test the theory
   - b) Identify the problem
   - c) Establish a plan
   - d) Document findings
2. Which of the following actions should be taken after establishing a theory of probable cause?
   - a) Ignore the theory
   - b) Document findings
   - c) Test the theory
   - d) Verify system functionality
3. What should you do if the theory is not confirmed during testing?
   - a) Establish a new theory
   - b) Skip to the next step
   - c) Ignore the problem
   - d) Document the issue
4. Why is it important to verify full system functionality after solving a problem?
   - a) To save time
   - b) To ensure the problem is truly resolved
   - c) To avoid documentation
   - d) To create more problems
5. What is the final step in the troubleshooting methodology?
   - a) Test the theory
   - b) Document findings and lessons learned
   - c) Establish a theory
   - d) Research the internet

Open Ended Questions: Answer the following questions in complete sentences:

1. Why is it important to establish a theory of probable cause during troubleshooting?

2. How can researching a knowledge base or the internet help in troubleshooting?

3. Explain why documenting findings and actions is beneficial after resolving a problem.

Answer Key:

Fill in the Blank:

1. identify
2. theory
3. research
4. resolve
5. verify

Multiple Choice Questions:

1. b) Identify the problem
2. c) Test the theory
3. a) Establish a new theory
4. b) To ensure the problem is truly resolved
5. b) Document findings and lessons learned

Open Ended Questions:

1. Establishing a theory of probable cause helps narrow down potential reasons for the problem, making it easier to test and resolve.
2. Researching a knowledge base or the internet can provide additional information, solutions, or similar cases that help in identifying and resolving the issue.
3. Documenting findings and actions is beneficial because it provides a record of what was done, which can help in preventing future issues and assist others facing similar problems.

CompTIA Fundamentals FC0-U71 Exam Preparation:

Domain 2 – Infrastructure

2.1 - Understanding Common Computing Devices

Computing devices are everywhere in our daily lives, and they serve various purposes. From staying connected to the internet to controlling our home environments, these devices make our lives easier and more efficient. Let's explore some common computing devices and their functions.

Fill in the Blank: Fill in the blank with the correct words.

1. _ are handheld devices that combine computing, telephone, and internet functions.
2. _ are portable computers that can be used on your lap.
3. _ is a type of computer designed for a single user to perform various tasks.
4. _ systems immerse users in a digital world, often used for gaming or simulations.
5. _ devices help manage energy use in homes, such as controlling heating and cooling.

Word bank: Tablets, Smartphones, Laptops, Virtual reality, Workstations, Thermostats

Multiple Choice Questions: Choose the correct answer from the choices for each question.

1. Which device is primarily used for reading digital books?
   - A) Laptop
   - B) E-reader
   - C) Gaming console
   - D) Server
2. What is the main purpose of a server?
   - A) To serve food at restaurants
   - B) To process data and provide services to other computers
   - C) To control home appliances
   - D) To play video games
3. Which device is used for enhancing the real world with digital information?
   - A) Augmented reality system
   - B) E-reader
   - C) Virtual reality system
   - D) Workstation
4. What kind of device is a Fitbit considered to be?
   - A) Home appliance
   - B) Medical device
   - C) Wearable device
   - D) Gaming console
5. Which device can be controlled remotely to lock and unlock doors?
   - A) Server
   - B) Laptop
   - C) Smart door lock
   - D) Gaming console

Open Ended Questions: Answer the following questions in complete sentences:

1. What are some benefits of using a tablet over a laptop?
2. How do smart home assistants improve daily life?

3. Describe a scenario where virtual reality could be beneficial outside of gaming.

Answer Key:

Fill in the Blank:

1. Smartphones
2. Laptops
3. Workstation
4. Virtual reality
5. Thermostats

Multiple Choice Questions:

1. B) E-reader
2. B) To process data and provide services to other computers
3. A) Augmented reality system
4. C) Wearable device
5. C) Smart door lock

Open Ended Questions: *(Example responses)*

1. Tablets are often lighter and more portable than laptops, making them easier to carry around. They also have longer battery life and are simpler for tasks like reading or browsing the web.
2. Smart home assistants can control various devices with voice commands, set reminders, play music, and provide information quickly, making daily tasks more convenient and hands-free.
3. Virtual reality can be beneficial in the field of education by providing immersive learning experiences, such as exploring historical sites or performing virtual science experiments, which can enhance understanding and engagement for students.

2.2 - Understanding Internal Computing Components

Computers are made up of various internal components that work together to perform tasks. Some of the most important components include the motherboard, which holds all the crucial parts of a computer and connects them; firmware, such as the BIOS, which helps start the computer; RAM, which temporarily stores data for quick access; the CPU, which performs calculations and tasks; and the GPU, which handles images and video. Storage devices save your data even when the computer is off. Network Interface Cards (NICs) allow computers to connect to networks either by wired or wireless connections. These components can be built into the motherboard (onboard) or added separately as expansion cards.

Fill in the Blank: Fill in the blank with the correct words.

1. The _ is the main circuit board that connects all components of a computer.
2. _ is a type of memory used to store data temporarily while the computer is on.
3. The _ is responsible for executing instructions and performing calculations.
4. _ stores data even when the computer is turned off.
5. A _ allows a computer to connect to a network.

Word bank: CPU, Network Interface Card, RAM, Storage, Motherboard

Multiple Choice Questions: Choose the correct answer from the choices for each question.

1. What component is responsible for rendering images and video?
   - a) BIOS
   - b) CPU
   - c) GPU
   - d) RAM
2. Which of the following is a function of the BIOS?
   - a) Store long-term data
   - b) Connect to the internet
   - c) Initialize hardware during startup
   - d) Execute applications
3. What type of data connection does a wired NIC use?
   - a) Bluetooth
   - b) Ethernet
   - c) Wi-Fi
   - d) Infrared
4. Which component would you upgrade to improve multitasking performance?
   - a) GPU
   - b) RAM
   - c) Storage
   - d) NIC
5. An expansion card is used to:
   - a) Increase the storage capacity
   - b) Add additional functionality like graphics or network capabilities
   - c) Improve the BIOS
   - d) Enhance the CPU speed

Open Ended Questions: Answer the following questions in complete sentences:

1. Explain the difference between onboard and expansion cards for network connectivity.

_____

2. How does the CPU and RAM work together to perform tasks on a computer?

_____

3. Describe the role of storage in a computer system.

_____

Answer Key:

Fill in the Blank:

1. Motherboard
2. RAM
3. CPU
4. Storage
5. Network Interface Card

Multiple Choice Questions:

1. c) GPU
2. c) Initialize hardware during startup
3. b) Ethernet
4. b) RAM
5. b) Add additional functionality like graphics or network capabilities

Open Ended Questions:

1. Onboard network cards are built into the motherboard, while expansion cards are separate components that can be added to enhance a computer's network capabilities.
2. The CPU processes instructions and tasks, while RAM provides quick access to data that the CPU needs to perform these tasks efficiently.
3. Storage in a computer system is used to save data and applications permanently, so they can be accessed and used even after the computer is turned off.

2.3 – Understanding Storage Types for CompTIA Fundamentals (FC0-U71) Exam

Storage devices are essential components of computing systems. They can be categorized as volatile and non-volatile, depending on whether they retain data when powered off. Local storage options include RAM, ROM, magnetic disks, solid-state drives, optical storage, and external flash drives. Additionally, storage can be network-based, such as Network-Attached Storage (NAS), file servers, or cloud storage.

Fill in the Blank: Fill in the blank with the correct words.

1. Volatile storage, such as _, loses its data when the power is turned off.
2. Non-volatile storage retains data without power, examples include _ *and* _.
3. _ is a type of storage that uses magnetic disks to store data.
4. A _ is a high-speed storage device that connects directly to the computer's motherboard.
5. Storage solutions like _ allow multiple users to access data over a network.

Word bank: Solid-state drive, RAM, ROM, Network-Attached Storage, Hard Disk Drive

Multiple Choice Questions: Choose the correct answer from the choices for each question.

1. Which of the following is a type of non-volatile storage?
   - A) RAM
   - B) SSD
   - C) Cache
   - D) CPU
2. What is the main advantage of a solid-state drive over a hard disk drive?
   - A) Larger storage capacity
   - B) Higher durability
   - C) Faster data access speed
   - D) Lower cost
3. Which type of storage is typically used for temporary data storage?
   - A) ROM
   - B) RAM
   - C) HDD
   - D) SSD
4. Which storage type is best for storing the BIOS of a computer?
   - A) RAM
   - B) SSD
   - C) ROM
   - D) HDD
5. What does NAS stand for in the context of storage?
   - A) Network-Attached System
   - B) Network-Attached Storage
   - C) Network Access Storage
   - D) Network Application System

Open Ended Questions: Answer the following questions in complete sentences:

1. Explain the difference between volatile and non-volatile storage with examples.
2. How does a solid-state drive improve the performance of a computer compared to a hard disk drive?
3. Describe a scenario where cloud storage might be more beneficial than local storage.

Answer Key:

Fill in the Blank:

1. RAM
2. ROM, SSD
3. Hard Disk Drive
4. Solid-state drive
5. Network-Attached Storage

Multiple Choice Questions:

1. B) SSD
2. C) Faster data access speed
3. B) RAM
4. C) ROM
5. B) Network-Attached Storage

Open Ended Questions:

1. Volatile storage, like RAM, loses its data when the power is turned off, while non-volatile storage, such as ROM and SSDs, retains data without power. RAM is used for temporary data during active processes, whereas ROM stores permanent instructions for the computer.
2. A solid-state drive improves computer performance by providing faster data access speeds, which reduces the time it takes to boot up and load applications compared to a hard disk drive that uses moving parts.
3. Cloud storage is beneficial in scenarios where data needs to be accessed from multiple locations, such as when collaborating on projects with team members across diff

2.4 –Installing and Configuring Peripheral Devices

In this worksheet, we will explore the installation and configuration of common peripheral devices, a key component of the CompTIA Fundamentals FC0-U71 Exam. Peripheral devices are external devices that connect to a computer to provide additional functionality. These devices include printers, scanners, keyboards, mice, web cameras, external drives, speakers/headsets, and various display options such as smart TVs, projectors, and monitors. Understanding the installation types, such as plug-n-play versus driver installation, and configuration steps for IP-based and web-based peripherals is essential.

Fill in the Blank: Fill in the blank with the correct words.

1. A __ is a peripheral device used to create a hard copy of digital documents.
2. To connect a mouse to a computer, you might use a __ connection, which typically requires no additional software.
3. A __ is used to input text and commands into a computer.
4. Before using a new printer, you may need to install a __ to ensure it functions correctly.
5. A __ is a device that can capture moving images and is often used for video calls.

Word bank: driver, keyboard, plug-n-play, web camera, printer

Multiple Choice Questions: Choose the correct answer from the choices for each question.

1. Which of the following devices is primarily used for scanning documents?
   - A) Keyboard
   - B) Printer
   - C) Scanner
   - D) Monitor
2. What type of power source can provide backup power in case of an electrical outage?
   - A) External drive
   - B) UPS (Uninterruptable Power Supply)
   - C) Mouse
   - D) Web camera
3. Which installation type typically requires you to download and install software from a manufacturer's website?
   - A) Plug-n-play
   - B) Driver installation
   - C) IP-based configuration
   - D) Web-based configuration
4. What is the primary use of a projector?
   - A) Printing documents
   - B) Displaying video on a large screen
   - C) Inputting text
   - D) Storing files
5. Which peripheral device might require an IP address for setup and configuration?
   - A) Keyboard
   - B) Monitor
   - C) Printer
   - D) Mouse

Open Ended Questions: Answer the following questions in complete sentences:

1. Explain the difference between plug-n-play and driver installation.

---

2. Describe a scenario where a web-based configuration might be necessary for a peripheral device.

---

3. Why is it important to understand the different types of peripheral devices and their installation procedures?

Answer Key:

Fill in the Blank:

1. printer
2. plug-n-play
3. keyboard
4. driver
5. web camera

Multiple Choice Questions:

1. C) Scanner
2. B) UPS (Uninterruptable Power Supply)
3. B) Driver installation
4. B) Displaying video on a large screen
5. C) Printer

Open Ended Questions:

1. Plug-n-play is a type of installation where the device is automatically recognized and configured by the operating system without needing additional software. Driver installation requires downloading and setting up specific software to enable the device's functionality.
2. A web-based configuration might be necessary when setting up a wireless printer. The configuration can be accessed through a web interface where you can adjust settings and connect the printer to a network.
3. Understanding the different types of peripheral devices and their installation procedures is important because it ensures that devices are properly connected and function as intended, which improves productivity and minimizes technical issues.

2.5 – Input/Output Device Interfaces

Understanding the various types of input/output device interfaces is crucial for setting up and managing computer systems efficiently. Input and output devices connect through different interfaces, which can be categorized into networking, peripheral devices, and display ports. Networking interfaces can be wired or wireless, each with specific connectors and standards. Peripheral devices often use USB or Bluetooth connections, while display ports vary from VGA to HDMI and more advanced types like USB-C.

Fill in the Blank: Fill in the blank with the correct words.

1. The Ethernet connector, also known as _, is commonly used for wired networking.
2. _ is a wireless technology that allows devices to communicate over short distances.
3. _ connectors are used to connect fiber optic cables in networking.
4. _ is a port that supports high-definition video and audio transfer.
5. Crimpers are tools used primarily for attaching _ to cables.

Word bank: HDMI, RJ45, SFP, Bluetooth, connectors

Multiple Choice Questions: Choose the correct answer from the choices for each question.

1. Which of the following is a wireless networking standard?
   - A) Ethernet
   - B) Bluetooth
   - C) USB
   - D) VGA
2. What type of connector does the Thunderbolt interface use?
   - A) USB-C
   - B) RJ45
   - C) DVI
   - D) HDMI
3. Which display port is considered legacy and typically used with older monitors?
   - A) HDMI
   - B) DisplayPort
   - C) VGA
   - D) USB-C
4. What is the primary purpose of a cable tester?
   - A) To connect devices
   - B) To test network cables for faults
   - C) To install software
   - D) To charge devices
5. Near-field communication (NFC) is often used in:
   - A) Large data transfers
   - B) Mobile payments
   - C) Video streaming
   - D) Home theater systems

Open Ended Questions: Answer the following questions in complete sentences:

1. Explain the difference between wired and wireless networking interfaces.
2. Describe the function of a USB-C port and where it might be used.
3. Discuss the benefits of using Bluetooth for connecting peripheral devices.

Answer Key:

Fill in the Blank:

1. RJ45
2. Bluetooth
3. SFP
4. HDMI
5. connectors

Multiple Choice Questions:

1. B) Bluetooth
2. A) USB-C
3. C) VGA
4. B) To test network cables for faults
5. B) Mobile payments

Open Ended Questions:

1. Wired networking interfaces use physical cables, such as Ethernet, to connect devices, providing a stable and often faster connection. Wireless networking interfaces, like Wi-Fi or Bluetooth, allow devices to connect without cables, offering greater flexibility and mobility.
2. A USB-C port is a versatile connector used for data transfer, charging, and video output. It is commonly found on modern laptops, smartphones, and tablets due to its ability to support high-speed data transfer and power delivery.
3. Bluetooth is beneficial for connecting peripheral devices because it eliminates the need for physical cables, allowing for a more organized workspace. It is energy-efficient and ideal for short-range connections, such as keyboards, mice, and headphones.

2.6 - Virtualization and Cloud Technologies

Virtualization and cloud technologies are essential concepts in modern computing. Virtualization refers to the process of creating a virtual version of something, such as a server or a desktop. This is often achieved using a hypervisor, which allows multiple guest operating systems to run on a single physical machine. Cloud technologies, on the other hand, involve delivering computing services over the internet. These services can include Platform as a Service (PaaS), Infrastructure as a Service (IaaS), and Software as a Service (SaaS). Deployment models for these technologies can vary, including on-premises, cloud, or hybrid solutions.

Fill in the Blank: Fill in the blank with the correct words.

1. A _ allows multiple guest operating systems to run on one physical machine.
2. _ as a Service provides a platform for developers to create applications online without managing the underlying hardware.
3. _ is the model where computing services are delivered over the internet.
4. An example of a _ deployment model would be a company using both on-premises servers and cloud servers.
5. _ as a Service allows users to access software applications over the internet without installing them locally.

Word bank: Hybrid, Hypervisor, Cloud, Software, Platform

Multiple Choice Questions: Choose the correct answer from the choices for each question.

1. What is the role of a hypervisor in virtualization?
   - A) To store data
   - B) To manage multiple operating systems on a single machine
   - C) To provide internet services
   - D) To run software applications
2. Which of the following is an example of Infrastructure as a Service (IaaS)?
   - A) Amazon Web Services (AWS)
   - B) Google Docs
   - C) Microsoft Windows
   - D) Adobe Photoshop
3. What is a primary benefit of using cloud technologies?
   - A) Requires more physical hardware
   - B) Reduces flexibility in software deployment
   - C) Provides scalable resources
   - D) Increases energy consumption
4. Which deployment model combines both on-premises and cloud resources?
   - A) On-premises
   - B) Cloud
   - C) Hybrid
   - D) Software
5. What type of service is provided by Software as a Service (SaaS)?
   - A) Hardware rental
   - B) Networking solutions
   - C) Online software access

- D) Data storage only

Open Ended Questions: Answer the following questions in complete sentences:

1. Explain the difference between virtualization and cloud technologies.

_____

_____

2. Describe a scenario where a hybrid deployment model would be beneficial.

_____

_____

3. Discuss the advantages of using Platform as a Service (PaaS) for developers.

_____

_____

Answer Key:

Fill in the Blank:

1. Hypervisor
2. Platform
3. Cloud
4. Hybrid
5. Software

Multiple Choice Questions:

1. B) To manage multiple operating systems on a single machine
2. A) Amazon Web Services (AWS)
3. C) Provides scalable resources
4. C) Hybrid
5. C) Online software access

Open Ended Questions:

1. Virtualization involves creating virtual versions of physical hardware, allowing multiple systems to run on a single machine using a hypervisor. Cloud technologies deliver services over the internet, providing scalable resources and reducing the need for physical hardware.
2. A hybrid deployment model would be beneficial for a company that wants to keep sensitive data secure on-premises while taking advantage of the scalability and flexibility of cloud services for less sensitive operations.

3. Platform as a Service (PaaS) offers developers an environment to build, test, and deploy applications without managing the underlying infrastructure. It allows for faster development cycles and scalability.

2.7 - Internet Service Types

The internet is an essential part of our daily lives, and various service types are available to connect us to the world. Understanding these types helps us choose the best service for our needs. Common internet service types include fiber optic, cable, digital subscriber line (DSL), and wireless options like RF, satellite, and cellular.

Fill in the Blank: Fill in the blank with the correct words.

1. _ internet uses light to transmit data and offers very high-speed connections.
2. _ internet is provided through coaxial cables and is widely available in urban areas.
3. _ is a type of internet service that uses telephone lines to transmit data.
4. _ internet service uses radio frequencies to connect users without physical cables.
5. _ internet can reach remote areas via a network of orbiting satellites.

Word bank: RF, DSL, Fiber optic, Cable, Satellite

Multiple Choice Questions: Choose the correct answer from the choices for each question.

1. Which internet service type typically offers the fastest speeds?
   - a) Cable
   - b) DSL
   - c) Fiber optic
   - d) Satellite
2. What type of internet service is commonly used in rural areas where cable or fiber is unavailable?
   - a) Cable
   - b) Satellite
   - c) DSL
   - d) Fiber optic
3. Which type of internet uses existing telephone lines for data transmission?
   - a) Cellular
   - b) Satellite
   - c) DSL
   - d) Fiber optic
4. RF internet service is primarily associated with which of the following?
   - a) Satellite
   - b) Wireless
   - c) Cable
   - d) DSL
5. Cellular internet service relies on which technology for data transmission?
   - a) Fiber optic cables
   - b) Radio frequencies
   - c) Telephone lines
   - d) Satellites

Open Ended Questions: Answer the following questions in complete sentences.

1. Explain the main advantage of fiber optic internet over other types.

---

2. Describe a scenario in which satellite internet would be the best option.

---

3. How does cellular internet service provide connectivity when traveling?

Answer Key:

Fill in the Blank:

1. Fiber optic
2. Cable
3. DSL
4. RF
5. Satellite

Multiple Choice Questions:

1. c) Fiber optic
2. b) Satellite
3. c) DSL
4. b) Wireless
5. b) Radio frequencies

Open Ended Questions:

1. Fiber optic internet provides faster speeds and more reliable connections than other types because it uses light for data transmission, reducing interference.
2. Satellite internet is ideal for remote locations where traditional cable or DSL services are unavailable, such as rural or mountainous areas.
3. Cellular internet service uses radio frequencies to connect to a network of cell towers, allowing users to access the internet while on the move.

2.8 - Basic Networking Concepts

Understanding basic networking concepts is essential for navigating the digital world. Networking involves various components and services that enable devices to communicate with each other. Key elements of networking include network communication basics, network identifiers like IP addresses and MAC addresses, and basic network services such as secure web browsing, file transfer, and email. Networking devices like modems, routers, switches, access points, and firewalls play significant roles in ensuring connectivity. Networking models, including client/server and peer-to-peer, describe how devices in a network communicate. Lastly, local area networks (LANs) and wide area networks (WANs) illustrate how networks can vary in size and coverage.

Fill in the Blank: Fill in the blank with the correct words.

1. An _ is a unique numerical label assigned to each device connected to a computer network.
2. A _ address is used to identify the physical hardware of a device in a network.
3. A _ allows computers to connect and communicate within a local area network.
4. A _ is used to secure the network by controlling incoming and outgoing traffic.
5. _ is a network model where each computer can act as a server for others.

Word bank: MAC, IP address, Firewall, Peer-to-peer, Switch

Multiple Choice Questions: Choose the correct answer from the choices for each question.

1. What device connects multiple networks and directs data between them?
   - A) Modem
   - B) Router
   - C) Switch
   - D) Access point
2. Which network service is used to send and receive messages over the internet?
   - A) File transfer
   - B) Secure web browsing
   - C) Email
   - D) Firewall
3. What is the primary function of a modem in a network?
   - A) To store data
   - B) To protect the network
   - C) To convert digital data to analog signals
   - D) To manage network traffic
4. Which type of network is typically used within a single building or campus?
   - A) WAN
   - B) MAN
   - C) LAN
   - D) PAN
5. Which of the following is not a function of a firewall?
   - A) Blocking unauthorized access
   - B) Monitoring network traffic
   - C) Encrypting data
   - D) Connecting devices to a network

Open Ended Questions: Answer the following questions in complete sentences:

1. Explain the difference between a client/server network and a peer-to-peer network.
2. Describe the role of a router in a network and how it differs from a switch.
3. How does secure web browsing protect internet users?

Answer Key:

Fill in the Blank:

1. IP address
2. MAC
3. Switch
4. Firewall
5. Peer-to-peer

Multiple Choice Questions:

1. B) Router
2. C) Email
3. C) To convert digital data to analog signals
4. C) LAN
5. C) Encrypting data

Open Ended Questions:

1. In a client/server network, one or more centralized servers provide resources and services to client computers. A peer-to-peer network does not have a centralized server; instead, each computer can provide resources and services to other computers directly.
2. A router is responsible for directing data packets between different networks, making sure they reach their destination efficiently. A switch, on the other hand, connects devices within the same network and forwards data to the correct device based on its MAC address.
3. Secure web browsing protects users by encrypting data exchanged between their browser and websites, preventing unauthorized access and data interception by third parties.

2.9 - Understanding Small Wireless Networks

Wireless networks are essential in connecting devices without physical cables. They use radio waves to transmit data, making them convenient for homes and businesses. The 802.11 standards, such as 802.11n, 802.11ac, and 802.11ax, define how these networks operate. These standards offer different speeds and capabilities, and are affected by interference and attenuation. Understanding the differences between older and newer standards, as well as the various frequency bands like 2.4GHz, 5GHz, and 6GHz, is crucial for setting up an efficient wireless network.

Fill in the Blank: Fill in the blank with the correct words.

1. The _ standard is known for offering faster speeds and better performance in wireless networks.
2. _ is a factor that can reduce the strength of a wireless signal as it passes through obstacles.
3. Older standards like 802.11n primarily operate on the _ band.
4. The 5GHz band is less crowded and has _ interference compared to the 2.4GHz band.
5. Newer standards such as 802.11ax can operate on the _ band, which is the newest addition for wireless frequencies.

Word bank: interference, 802.11ax, 2.4GHz, less, attenuation

Multiple Choice Questions: Choose the correct answer from the choices for each question.

1. Which of the following is a characteristic of the 802.11ac standard?
   - A) Operates only on the 2.4GHz band
   - B) Provides slower speeds than 802.11n
   - C) Offers faster speeds and operates on the 5GHz band
   - D) Is the same as 802.11b
2. What is a common issue that affects wireless network performance due to physical obstacles?
   - A) Speed
   - B) Attenuation
   - C) Frequency
   - D) Bandwidth
3. Which frequency band is known for having more channels and less interference?
   - A) 2.4GHz
   - B) 5GHz
   - C) 1GHz
   - D) 10GHz
4. The 6GHz band is primarily associated with which 802.11 standard?
   - A) 802.11n
   - B) 802.11ac
   - C) 802.11ax
   - D) 802.11a
5. Why might someone choose to use the 2.4GHz band?
   - A) It is less crowded.
   - B) It has more range and penetrates walls better.
   - C) It is faster than the 5GHz band.

- D) It supports the 802.11ax standard.

Open Ended Questions: Answer the following questions in complete sentences:

1. Explain the advantages of using the 802.11ax standard in a home network.
2. How does interference impact the performance of a wireless network, and what can be done to minimize it?
3. Compare the 2.4GHz and 5GHz frequency bands in terms of their strengths and weaknesses for wireless networking.

Answer Key:
Fill in the Blank:

1. 802.11ax
2. Attenuation
3. 2.4GHz
4. Less
5. 6GHz

Multiple Choice Questions:

1. C) Offers faster speeds and operates on the 5GHz band
2. B) Attenuation
3. B) 5GHz
4. C) 802.11ax
5. B) It has more range and penetrates walls better.

Open Ended Questions:

1. The 802.11ax standard provides faster speeds, better performance, and can handle more devices simultaneously, which makes it ideal for a busy home network with multiple users and devices.
2. Interference from other devices, walls, and electronic equipment can weaken wireless signals, leading to slower speeds and dropped connections. To minimize interference, users can place their router in a central location, use the 5GHz band, and reduce the number of devices that use the same frequency.
3. The 2.4GHz band has a longer range and better wall penetration, making it suitable for larger areas. However, it is more crowded and prone to interference. The 5GHz band offers faster speeds and less interference but has a shorter range and is less effective at penetrating walls.

CompTIA Fundamentals FC0-U71 Exam Preparation:

Domain 3 – Applications and Software

3.1 – Understanding Operating Systems

Operating systems (OS) are essential components of computers, managing hardware and software resources. They provide a user interface, manage files, and facilitate applications. This worksheet will help you understand key OS components, including file management and system utilities.

Fill in the Blank: Fill in the blank with the correct words.

1. The __ is the part of the OS that manages files and directories.
2. __ is a feature that reduces the size of files to save space.
3. __ is a process that converts data into a secure format to prevent unauthorized access.
4. The __ is a text-based interface where users can type commands to interact with the OS.
5. File __ define the access level and operations that can be performed on files and directories.

Word bank: encryption, compression, permissions, filesystem, console/command line

Multiple Choice Questions: Choose the correct answer from the choices for each question.

1. What is the primary purpose of an operating system?
   - A) To provide a platform for hardware
   - B) To manage software applications
   - C) To manage hardware and software resources
   - D) To offer internet connectivity
2. Which of the following is a graphical user interface (GUI) element?
   - A) Command Prompt
   - B) Terminal
   - C) Icons and Windows
   - D) Script Editor
3. What file extension is commonly used for text files?
   - A) .exe
   - B) .txt
   - C) .jpg
   - D) .pdf
4. Which of these is not a system utility?
   - A) Disk Cleanup
   - B) Antivirus Software
   - C) Web Browser
   - D) Backup Tool
5. What does a driver in an OS do?
   - A) Provides security updates
   - B) Controls hardware devices
   - C) Manages network connections
   - D) Supports software development

Open Ended Questions: Answer the following questions in complete sentences:

1. Describe the difference between a folder and a directory.

2. Explain why file permissions are important in an operating system.

3. Discuss the advantages of using a graphical user interface (GUI) over a console/command line interface.

Answer Key:

Fill in the Blank:

1. filesystem
2. Compression
3. Encryption
4. console/command line
5. permissions

Multiple Choice Questions:

1. C) To manage hardware and software resources
2. C) Icons and Windows
3. B) .txt
4. C) Web Browser
5. B) Controls hardware devices

Open Ended Questions:

1. A folder is a graphical representation of a directory, which is a structure that contains files and other directories. They both help organize files on a computer.
2. File permissions are important because they control who can read, write, or execute a file, ensuring security and proper access management.
3. A graphical user interface (GUI) is often easier to use because it allows users to interact with the system through visual elements like icons and windows, rather than typing commands, making it more user-friendly for most people.

3.2 – Understanding Operating Systems

Operating systems (OS) are essential software that manage computer hardware and software resources, providing common services for computer programs. They act as an intermediary between users and the computer hardware, enabling applications to run smoothly. Key functions of an operating system include disk management, task and process management, application management, device management, and access control. Different types of operating systems are designed for various devices, such as mobile devices, desktops/workstations, servers, and embedded systems.

Fill in the Blank: Fill in the blank with the correct words.

1. An operating system serves as an _ between applications and hardware.
2. _ management involves organizing and keeping track of files and storage on disk drives.
3. Operating systems help in _ control by managing user permissions and access rights.
4. A _ operating system is designed for use on smartphones and tablets.
5. _ management in an OS allows for running multiple applications simultaneously.

Word bank: device, disk, interface, mobile, access, task

Multiple Choice Questions: Choose the correct answer from the choices for each question.

1. Which of the following is NOT a type of operating system?
   - A) Mobile device OS
   - B) Desktop/workstation OS
   - C) Calculator OS
   - D) Server OS
2. What is the main role of an operating system's task manager?
   - A) To provide internet access
   - B) To manage running applications and processes
   - C) To increase computer speed
   - D) To protect against viruses
3. Which OS type is commonly used in industrial machines and appliances?
   - A) Mobile OS
   - B) Desktop OS
   - C) Embedded OS
   - D) Server OS
4. What does application management in an operating system involve?
   - A) Managing hardware components
   - B) Installing, updating, and uninstalling software
   - C) Providing cloud storage
   - D) Monitoring internet usage
5. Which of the following is a function of device management in an operating system?
   - A) Managing user accounts
   - B) Controlling peripheral devices like printers and scanners
   - C) Providing email services
   - D) Designing user interfaces

Open Ended Questions: Answer the following questions in complete sentences:

1. Explain how operating systems manage access control for users.
2. Describe the differences between a server OS and a desktop OS.
3. Why is disk management an important function of an operating system?

Answer Key:

Fill in the Blank:

1. interface
2. Disk
3. access
4. Mobile
5. Task

Multiple Choice Questions:

1. C) Calculator OS
2. B) To manage running applications and processes
3. C) Embedded OS
4. B) Installing, updating, and uninstalling software
5. B) Controlling peripheral devices like printers and scanners

Open Ended Questions:

1. Operating systems manage access control by setting permissions for different users. This ensures that only authorized users can access certain files and applications, enhancing security.
2. A server OS is designed to manage network resources and serve multiple users simultaneously, whereas a desktop OS is designed for single-user operations with a focus on user-friendly interfaces and applications.
3. Disk management is crucial because it helps organize data, manage space efficiently, and maintain the health of storage devices, ensuring data is stored and retrieved reliably.

3.3 – Understanding Software

Software plays a crucial role in making computers useful. It allows us to perform various tasks, such as creating documents, analyzing data, and communicating with others. Understanding different types of software and their purposes is essential for using technology effectively.

Fill in the Blank: Fill in the blank with the correct words.

1. _ software is used to create documents, such as letters and reports.
2. A _ is a type of productivity software used to organize data in rows and columns.
3. _ software allows people to send and receive messages over the internet.
4. _ is a type of collaboration software that helps teams work together on shared documents.
5. _ is used to browse websites and access information online.

Word bank: Email client, Spreadsheet, Web-browsing, Word processing, Document sharing

Multiple Choice Questions: Choose the correct answer from the choices for each question.

1. Which software is primarily used for creating presentations?
   - A. Visual diagramming
   - B. Word processing
   - C. Spreadsheet
   - D. Presentation
2. What type of software is used for online meetings and video calls?
   - A. Email client
   - B. Conferencing
   - C. Document sharing
   - D. Instant messaging
3. Which of the following is an example of collaboration software?
   - A. Spreadsheet
   - B. Presentation
   - C. Online workspace
   - D. Web-browsing
4. What is the main purpose of instant messaging software?
   - A. To edit documents
   - B. To send quick text messages
   - C. To create diagrams
   - D. To analyze data
5. Remote support software is mainly used for:
   - A. Creating spreadsheets
   - B. Assisting users with technical issues
   - C. Designing presentations
   - D. Browsing the internet

Open Ended Questions: Answer the following questions in complete sentences:

1. Explain how productivity software can help you in your schoolwork.

2. Describe a scenario where collaboration software would be useful.
3. What are some benefits of using web-browsing software?

Answer Key:

Fill in the Blank:

1. Word processing
2. Spreadsheet
3. Email client
4. Document sharing
5. Web-browsing

Multiple Choice Questions:

1. D. Presentation
2. B. Conferencing
3. C. Online workspace
4. B. To send quick text messages
5. B. Assisting users with technical issues

Open Ended Questions:

1. Productivity software can help in schoolwork by allowing students to create essays and reports, organize data in spreadsheets for projects, and make presentations for class assignments. It helps in presenting information clearly and efficiently.
2. Collaboration software would be useful in a group project where team members need to work on the same document from different locations. It allows them to share files, communicate, and make edits in real-time, ensuring everyone is on the same page.
3. Some benefits of using web-browsing software include access to a wide range of information for research, the ability to connect with educational resources, and the convenience of finding answers to questions quickly. It also enables students to explore topics beyond their textbooks.

3.4 – Configuring Web Browser Features

The CompTIA IT Fundamentals (FC0-U71) exam covers the essential concepts of computing, IT infrastructure, software development, and database use. For this worksheet, we'll focus on configuring and using web browser features. Understanding these features is crucial for efficient and secure web browsing.

Fill in the Blank: Fill in the blank with the correct words.

1. To browse the internet without saving your history, you should use _ browsing.
2. Browser _ or extensions can be added to enhance functionality.
3. To manage stored website data and improve performance, regularly clear your browser's _.
4. A _ blocker helps prevent unwanted advertisements from appearing.
5. Use profile _ to keep your bookmarks and settings consistent across devices.

Word bank: synchronization, cache, pop-up, add-ons, private

Multiple Choice Questions: Choose the correct answer from the choices for each question.

1. Which of the following is used to prevent advertisements from appearing on your screen?
   - a) History
   - b) Cache
   - c) Pop-up blocker
   - d) Extension
2. What is the main purpose of using private browsing?
   - a) To speed up browsing
   - b) To hide browsing history
   - c) To save bookmarks
   - d) To enable extensions
3. Which action can be performed to improve browser performance?
   - a) Enabling pop-ups
   - b) Clearing cache
   - c) Disabling bookmarks
   - d) Synchronizing profiles
4. What feature allows you to keep the same bookmarks and settings across multiple devices?
   - a) Cache management
   - b) Profile synchronization
   - c) Pop-up blockers
   - d) Default search engine
5. Which of these can be added to a browser to extend its functionality?
   - a) Cache
   - b) Pop-up blocker
   - c) Add-ons/extensions
   - d) Private browsing

Open Ended Questions: Answer the following questions in complete sentences:

1. Explain the benefits of using browser add-ons or extensions.

_____

2. Why is it important to clear your browser's cache regularly?

_____

3. Describe how profile synchronization can be useful for users with multiple devices.

_____

Answer Key:

Fill in the Blank:

1. private
2. add-ons
3. cache
4. pop-up
5. synchronization

Multiple Choice Questions:

1. c) Pop-up blocker
2. b) To hide browsing history
3. b) Clearing cache
4. b) Profile synchronization
5. c) Add-ons/extensions

Open Ended Questions:

1. Browser add-ons or extensions provide additional features that can enhance functionality, such as ad-blocking, password management, or productivity tools.
2. Clearing your browser's cache is important because it frees up space and ensures that you are viewing the most current version of web pages.
3. Profile synchronization is useful for maintaining consistent bookmarks and settings across multiple devices, ensuring a seamless browsing experience.

3.5 – Understanding AI

Artificial Intelligence (AI) is a branch of computer science that aims to create machines that can perform tasks typically requiring human intelligence. AI has various applications in daily life, such as AI chatbots, AI assistants, generative AI, and AI predictions and suggestions.

Fill in the Blank: Fill in the blank with the correct words.

1. An AI _ can hold conversations with users and provide customer support.
2. AI _ like Siri and Alexa help users manage tasks and answer questions.
3. _ AI can create new content, such as texts or images.
4. AI-generated _ can assist programmers by providing code snippets.
5. _ and suggestions help improve user experience by predicting what users might want or need.

Word bank: predictions, chatbots, assistants, content, generative

Multiple Choice Questions: Choose the correct answer from the choices for each question.

1. What is the main purpose of an AI chatbot?
   - a) To generate code
   - b) To hold conversations with users
   - c) To manage household appliances
   - d) To create new music
2. Which of these is an example of an AI assistant?
   - a) Google Search
   - b) Microsoft Word
   - c) Siri
   - d) Spotify
3. What type of AI is used to generate new content?
   - a) Predictive AI
   - b) Analytical AI
   - c) Generative AI
   - d) Reactive AI
4. How can AI-generated code be beneficial to programmers?
   - a) By creating complete software programs
   - b) By providing code snippets and suggestions
   - c) By fixing all bugs automatically
   - d) By replacing programmers completely
5. What is the role of AI predictions and suggestions?
   - a) To entertain users
   - b) To improve user experience
   - c) To replace human decision-making
   - d) To eliminate the need for human input

Open Ended Questions: Answer the following questions in complete sentences:

1. Describe how AI chatbots are used in customer service.
2. Explain the benefits of using AI assistants in everyday life.
3. Discuss the potential impact of generative AI on creative industries.

Answer Key:

Fill in the Blank:

1. chatbots
2. assistants
3. Generative
4. content
5. Predictions

Multiple Choice Questions:

1. b) To hold conversations with users
2. c) Siri
3. c) Generative AI
4. b) By providing code snippets and suggestions
5. b) To improve user experience

Open Ended Questions:

1. AI chatbots are used in customer service to interact with customers, answer their inquiries, and provide support, often improving efficiency and availability of services.
2. AI assistants help users by managing tasks such as setting reminders, answering questions, and controlling smart home devices, making everyday life more convenient and organized.
3. Generative AI has the potential to transform creative industries by enabling the creation of new art, music, and literature. It can inspire artists by providing new ideas and expand the possibilities of creative expression. However, it also raises questions about originality and authorship.

CompTIA Fundamentals FC0-U71 Exam Preparation:

Domain 4 – Software Development Concepts

4.1 – Programming Language Categories

Programming languages can be categorized into various types based on their functionality and purpose. **Interpreted languages** are executed line by line, which includes scripting and markup languages. **Scripting languages** are used for writing scripts that automate tasks, while **markup languages** like HTML are used to define the structure of data. **Compiled programming languages** are transformed into machine code before execution, leading to faster performance. **Query languages** are used to make queries in databases, and **assembly languages** are low-level languages that are closer to machine code.

Fill in the Blank: Fill in the blank with the correct words.

1. _ languages are executed line by line and include scripting and markup languages.
2. HTML is an example of a _ language used to define the structure of data.
3. _ languages are transformed into machine code before execution.
4. _ languages are used to automate tasks through scripts.
5. SQL is an example of a _ language used for making database queries.

Word bank: assembly, scripting, compiled, markup, interpreted, query

Multiple Choice Questions: Choose the correct answer from the choices for each question.

1. Which type of language is HTML?
   a) Compiled
   b) Scripting
   c) Markup
   d) Query
2. What is the main characteristic of compiled languages?
   a) Executed line by line
   b) Transformed into machine code
   c) Used for web pages
   d) Used for database queries
3. Which language is closest to machine code?
   a) Scripting
   b) Assembly
   c) Markup
   d) Query
4. What kind of language is SQL?
   a) Interpreted
   b) Query
   c) Compiled
   d) Markup
5. Which language is typically used for writing scripts to automate tasks?
   a) Assembly
   b) Scripting
   c) Compiled
   d) Query

Open Ended Questions: Answer the following questions in complete sentences:

1. Explain the difference between scripting and markup languages.
2. Why are compiled languages generally faster than interpreted languages?
3. How do query languages interact with databases?

Answer Key:

Fill in the Blank:

1. Interpreted
2. Markup
3. Compiled
4. Scripting
5. Query

Multiple Choice Questions:

1. c) Markup
2. b) Transformed into machine code
3. b) Assembly
4. b) Query
5. b) Scripting

Open Ended Questions:

1. Scripting languages are used for writing scripts that automate tasks, while markup languages, like HTML, are used to define the structure and presentation of data.
2. Compiled languages are generally faster because they are converted into machine code before execution, which allows for more efficient processing by the computer's CPU compared to interpreted languages that are executed line by line.
3. Query languages, like SQL, interact with databases by allowing users to retrieve, update, and manage data through queries written in the language.

4.2 – Understanding Data Types

Data types are fundamental to programming and understanding how computers process information. In this section, we'll explore some basic data types and their characteristics. These include characters (char), strings, numbers (both integers and floats), and Boolean values.

- **Char**: Represents a single character, like 'a' or '5'.
- **Strings**: A sequence of characters, such as "hello" or "12345".
- **Numbers**:
    - **Integers**: Whole numbers, such as 33, $-5-5$, or 4242.
    - **Floats**: Numbers with decimals, like $3.143.14$, $-0.001-0.001$, or $2.02.0$.
- **Boolean**: Represents true or false values.

Fill in the Blank: Fill in the blank with the correct words.

1. A _ is a single character, such as 'A' or '9'.
2. A _ can hold a sequence of characters, like "Hello World".
3. An _ is a whole number without any decimal point.
4. A _ is a number that can have a decimal point.
5. A _ value can only be true or false.

Word bank: Boolean, Float, Integer, Char, String

Multiple Choice Questions: Choose the correct answer from the choices for each question.

1. What data type would you use to store someone's first name?
    - A) Char
    - B) String
    - C) Integer
    - D) Boolean
2. Which of the following is an example of a float?
    - A) 1212
    - B) 3.53.5
    - C) "3.5"
    - D) True
3. What data type is used to represent true or false values?
    - A) Integer
    - B) String
    - C) Boolean
    - D) Char
4. If you want to store the number of students in a class, which data type is most appropriate?
    - A) Float
    - B) String
    - C) Char
    - D) Integer
5. Which data type can store the value 'G'?
    - A) Integer

- B) Float
- C) Char
- D) Boolean

Open Ended Questions: Answer the following questions in complete sentences:

1. Explain the difference between an integer and a float.

2. Why is it important to choose the correct data type when programming?

3. Give an example of when you might use a Boolean data type in a computer program.

Answer Key:

Fill in the Blank:

1. Char
2. String
3. Integer
4. Float
5. Boolean

Multiple Choice Questions:

1. B) String
2. B) 3.53.5
3. C) Boolean
4. D) Integer
5. C) Char

Open Ended Questions:

1. An integer is a whole number without a decimal point, while a float is a number that can have decimal points for more precision.
2. Choosing the correct data type is important because it affects how data is stored, processed, and what operations can be performed on it.
3. A Boolean data type might be used in a program to check conditions, such as whether a user is logged in (true) or not (false).

4.3 – Understanding Programming Concepts

Programming is the process of creating a set of instructions for computers to perform specific tasks. In this worksheet, we will explore key programming concepts such as identifiers, variables, constants, arrays, functions, and objects which include properties, attributes, and methods. Understanding these concepts is essential for developing efficient and effective software.

Fill in the Blank: Fill in the blank with the correct words.

1. A _ is a name given to a memory location used to store data that can change during program execution.
2. A _ is a fixed value that does not change during the execution of a program.
3. An _ is a collection of elements, all of the same type, accessible by an index.
4. A _ is a block of code designed to perform a particular task and is called upon to execute when needed.
5. The _ of an object refer to the characteristics or data contained within that object.

Word bank: variables, constants, attributes, arrays, function

Multiple Choice Questions: Choose the correct answer from the choices for each question.

1. What is the purpose of a variable in programming?
   - a) To store a fixed value
   - b) To perform a specific task
   - c) To store data that can change
   - d) To define a collection of elements
2. Which of the following is used to store multiple values under a single name?
   - a) Variable
   - b) Function
   - c) Array
   - d) Constant
3. What is a method in the context of programming objects?
   - a) A variable that stores data
   - b) A function that defines an object's behavior
   - c) A constant value
   - d) An attribute of an object
4. How are elements in an array accessed?
   - a) By using a variable name
   - b) By using an index
   - c) By calling a function
   - d) By using a constant
5. What defines an object's characteristics?
   - a) Methods
   - b) Functions
   - c) Attributes
   - d) Variables

Open Ended Questions: Answer the following questions in complete sentences:

1. Describe the difference between a variable and a constant in programming.
2. Explain how a function can be useful in a program.
3. How do properties and attributes relate to objects in programming?

Answer Key:

Fill in the Blank:

1. variable
2. constant
3. array
4. function
5. attributes

Multiple Choice Questions:

1. c) To store data that can change
2. c) Array
3. b) A function that defines an object's behavior
4. b) By using an index
5. c) Attributes

Open Ended Questions:

1. **Example Response**: A variable is used to store data that can change during the execution of a program, while a constant is used to store a fixed value that remains the same throughout the program.
2. **Example Response**: A function is useful in a program because it allows a specific task to be performed when called, making the program more organized and reusable.
3. **Example Response**: Properties and attributes of an object define its characteristics or data it contains. They are essential for describing the object's state and behavior.

4.4 – Programming Organizational Techniques and Logic Concepts

Understanding programming involves learning how to organize code and use logic to solve problems. In this worksheet, we explore organizational techniques like pseudocode, object-oriented methods, comments, documentation, and flowchart concepts. Additionally, we'll cover logic concepts such as branching and looping.

Fill in the Blank: Fill in the blank with the correct words.

1. A _ is a simplified version of programming code, used to plan out the steps of an algorithm.
2. _ programming involves creating "objects" that combine data and functions.
3. Adding _ to code helps other programmers understand what the code does.
4. A _ chart is a visual representation of the steps in a process.
5. In a flowchart, a _ represents a decision point where branching occurs.

Word bank: comments, object-oriented, pseudocode, flow, sequence

Multiple Choice Questions: Choose the correct answer from the choices for each question.

1. What is the purpose of pseudocode?
   - a) To execute programs directly
   - b) To plan and outline a program before coding
   - c) To replace actual programming languages
   - d) To debug code
2. In object-oriented programming, an "object" is:
   - a) A standalone program
   - b) A collection of data and methods
   - c) A type of database
   - d) Only used for graphics
3. Which symbol in a flowchart represents a decision?
   - a) Oval
   - b) Rectangle
   - c) Diamond
   - d) Circle
4. What is the main purpose of comments in code?
   - a) To increase the file size
   - b) To execute special commands
   - c) To make the code run faster
   - d) To explain and clarify the code for humans
5. Which logic concept involves repeating a set of instructions?
   - a) Branching
   - b) Looping
   - c) Sequencing
   - d) Terminating

Open Ended Questions: Answer the following questions in complete sentences:

1. Explain why using comments in your code is important.

_____

_____

2. Describe a scenario where you might use a loop in a program.

_____

_____

3. How can flowcharts be beneficial in the planning stage of programming?

_____

_____

Answer Key:

Fill in the Blank:

1. pseudocode
2. object-oriented
3. comments
4. flow
5. sequence

Multiple Choice Questions:

1. b) To plan and outline a program before coding
2. b) A collection of data and methods
3. c) Diamond
4. d) To explain and clarify the code for humans
5. b) Looping

Open Ended Questions:

1. Using comments in your code is important because they help explain the purpose and functionality of different parts of the code, making it easier for others to understand and maintain it.
2. A loop might be used in a program to repeatedly execute a block of code, such as processing each item in a list or repeating a task until a condition is met.
3. Flowcharts can be beneficial in the planning stage of programming because they provide a visual representation of the steps involved in a process, helping identify potential issues and ensuring a clear understanding of the program's structure.

CompTIA Fundamentals FC0-U71 Exam Preparation:

Domain 5 – Data and Database Fundamentals

5.1 – Understanding Data and Information

In today's digital age, data and information are valuable assets. They help businesses make informed decisions and gain insights into their operations. Critical data is essential for the functioning of a company, while non-critical data, although useful, is not vital for immediate decision-making. Businesses capture and collect data to analyze it for meaningful reporting and data-driven decisions. Data monetization involves turning data into revenue, while data analytics and Big Data help in understanding large sets of information.

Fill in the Blank: Fill in the blank with the correct words.

1. Data and information are considered valuable _ for businesses.
2. _ data is necessary for the immediate operation of a company, while non-critical data is not.
3. Businesses use data capture and _ to gather necessary information.
4. Data _ involves converting data into revenue or profit.
5. _ analytics helps businesses understand large sets of information.

Word bank: monetization, critical, assets, collection, Data

Multiple Choice Questions: Choose the correct answer from the choices for each question.

1. What is the primary purpose of data-driven business decisions?
   - A) To ignore data
   - B) To analyze and use data for informed decision-making
   - C) To reduce data collection
   - D) To increase data storage
2. What is an example of critical data?
   - A) Employee lunch preferences
   - B) Financial records essential for audits
   - C) Office decoration styles
   - D) Employee birthdays
3. What does data monetization mean?
   - A) Destroying data
   - B) Ignoring data
   - C) Turning data into revenue
   - D) Storing data indefinitely
4. How does data analytics benefit a business?
   - A) It increases the amount of data stored
   - B) It decreases customer engagement
   - C) It helps in understanding patterns and trends
   - D) It reduces data accuracy
5. What is Big Data?
   - A) Small amounts of data
   - B) Large volumes of data that can be analyzed for insights
   - C) Data that is ignored
   - D) Data that is deleted regularly

Open Ended Questions: Answer the following questions in complete sentences:

1. Explain why data and information are considered assets for businesses.

_____

_____

2. Describe the process of data capture and collection.

_____

_____

3. How can businesses use data analytics to improve their operations?

_____

_____

Answer Key:

Fill in the Blank:

1. assets
2. Critical
3. collection
4. monetization
5. Data

Multiple Choice Questions:

1. B) To analyze and use data for informed decision-making
2. B) Financial records essential for audits
3. C) Turning data into revenue
4. C) It helps in understanding patterns and trends
5. B) Large volumes of data that can be analyzed for insights

Open Ended Questions:

1. Data and information are considered assets for businesses because they provide valuable insights that can help in making informed decisions, improving efficiency, and gaining a competitive edge in the market.
2. Data capture and collection involve gathering relevant information from various sources, such as customer interactions, sales transactions, and online activities, to be analyzed and used for business insights.
3. Businesses can use data analytics to improve their operations by identifying trends and patterns, optimizing processes, enhancing customer experiences, and making data-driven decisions that lead to better outcomes.

5.2 – Understanding Database Concepts

Databases are essential tools in the modern world, helping organize and manage data efficiently. A database is a structured set of data held in a computer, especially one that is accessible in various ways. Databases allow users to create, import, query, and generate reports from data. They differ from flat files by supporting multiple concurrent users, offering scalability, speed, and handling a variety of data types. Understanding database records, storage, data persistence, and availability are crucial for those preparing for IT exams like the CompTIA Fundamentals FC0-U71.

Fill in the Blank: Fill in the blank with the correct words.

1. The purpose of a database is to store and manage _ efficiently.
2. A _ file can have many users accessing it at the same time.
3. Databases are designed to provide data _ and ensure data is available when needed.
4. _ allows users to extract and manipulate data from a database.
5. Data _ refers to the ability of data to remain intact over time.

Word bank: availability, query, data, persistence, database

Multiple Choice Questions: Choose the correct answer from the choices for each question.

1. What is the main advantage of using a database over a flat file?
   - A) Only one user can access it
   - B) Supports a variety of data types
   - C) Slower speed
   - D) Data is not organized
2. Which of the following is NOT a database use?
   - A) Import
   - B) Query
   - C) Print
   - D) Reports
3. How does cloud storage differ from local storage?
   - A) Cloud storage is always offline
   - B) Cloud storage offers limited scalability
   - C) Cloud storage allows access from any internet-connected device
   - D) Local storage is more secure than any cloud option
4. What does data persistence ensure in a database?
   - A) Data is temporarily available
   - B) Data remains available and intact over time
   - C) Data can be accessed by only one person
   - D) Data is constantly changing
5. Which of the following is an example of data availability?
   - A) Data is deleted after use
   - B) Data can be accessed both online and offline
   - C) Data is only available during work hours
   - D) Data is stored in a single location

Open Ended Questions: Answer the following questions in complete sentences:

1. Explain the difference between a flat file and a database.
2. Describe a scenario where data persistence is important in a database.
3. How does the ability to query a database benefit businesses?

Answer Key:

Fill in the Blank:

1. data
2. database
3. availability
4. Query
5. persistence

Multiple Choice Questions:

1. B) Supports a variety of data types
2. C) Print
3. C) Cloud storage allows access from any internet-connected device
4. B) Data remains available and intact over time
5. B) Data can be accessed both online and offline

Open Ended Questions:

1. A flat file is a simple database where data is stored in a single table, whereas a database can have multiple tables linked together, allowing for complex data relationships and more efficient data management.
2. Data persistence is important in scenarios like financial record keeping or patient medical histories, where it is crucial that data remains unchanged and accessible over time to ensure accuracy and reliability.
3. Querying a database allows businesses to quickly retrieve specific information, such as sales data or customer records, which can aid in decision-making and strategic planning.

5.3 – Database Structures

Databases are essential for storing, organizing, and managing data. Understanding the different types of database structures is crucial for IT professionals. Databases can be classified into structured, semistructured, and non-structured types. Structured databases, like relational databases, are organized into tables with rows and columns. Semistructured databases have some organizational structure but are more flexible. Non-structured databases, such as document or key/value databases, allow for unstructured data storage.

Fill in the Blank: Fill in the blank with the correct words.

1. A _ database organizes data into tables, which consist of rows and columns.
2. In a relational database, a _ key uniquely identifies each row in a table.
3. A _ database stores data in key-value pairs.
4. _ databases allow for the storage of unstructured data, often using a flexible format like JSON.
5. A _ in a table is a single data point, such as a name or ID number.

Word bank: rows, relational, document, primary, key/value

Multiple Choice Questions: Choose the correct answer from the choices for each question.

1. Which of the following is an example of a structured database?
   - a) Key/value database
   - b) Relational database
   - c) Document database
   - d) Graph database
2. What term describes a column in a database table?
   - a) Record
   - b) Field
   - c) Key
   - d) Value
3. Which key in a relational database can link tables together?
   - a) Primary key
   - b) Secondary key
   - c) Foreign key
   - d) Composite key
4. What type of database uses a flexible format to store data, such as JSON?
   - a) Relational database
   - b) Key/value database
   - c) Document database
   - d) Hierarchical database
5. Which of the following is NOT a characteristic of a non-relational database?
   - a) Uses tables
   - b) Stores data in a flexible format
   - c) Suitable for unstructured data
   - d) Often uses key-value pairs

Open Ended Questions: Answer the following questions in complete sentences:

1. Explain the difference between a primary key and a foreign key in a relational database.

   _____

2. Describe a scenario where a document database might be more suitable than a relational database.

   _____

3. How do constraints in a relational database help maintain data integrity?

   _____

Answer Key:

Fill in the Blank:

1. relational
2. primary
3. key/value
4. document
5. row

Multiple Choice Questions:

1. b) Relational database
2. b) Field
3. c) Foreign key
4. c) Document database
5. a) Uses tables

Open Ended Questions:

1. A primary key is a unique identifier for each row in a table, ensuring no two rows have the same key value. A foreign key is a field in one table that links to the primary key of another table, establishing a relationship between the two tables.
2. A document database might be more suitable than a relational database when dealing with large volumes of unstructured data, such as user comments or blog posts, where each entry can vary significantly in structure.
3. Constraints in a relational database, such as primary key, foreign key, and unique constraints, help maintain data integrity by ensuring that the data entered into the database adheres to specific rules and relationships, preventing errors and inconsistencies.

5.4 – Basic Data Backup Concepts

In today's digital world, data backups are crucial. They ensure that important files, system settings, and personal data are not lost due to unexpected events like hardware failures or cyber-attacks. There are different types of backups, such as file backups and system backups. File backups involve saving copies of individual files, while system backups involve creating a snapshot of the entire system, including the operating system and installed applications.

Data can be stored in various locations. Locally, it can be kept on devices like flash drives, external hard drives, or Secure Digital (SD) cards. Another option is cloud storage, which allows data to be stored on remote servers and accessed via the internet. Cloud storage offers benefits like easy access from anywhere and protection against local hardware failures.

Fill in the Blank: Fill in the blank with the correct words.

1. A _ backup involves saving copies of individual files.
2. A _ backup creates a snapshot of the entire system.
3. _ storage allows data to be accessed via the internet.
4. A _ drive is a portable storage device used for local backups.
5. _ failures can result in data loss if there are no backups.

Word bank: cloud, flash, file, system, hardware

Multiple Choice Questions: Choose the correct answer from the choices for each question.

1. What is the main advantage of using cloud storage?
   - A) It is more expensive than local storage.
   - B) It offers protection against local hardware failures.
   - C) It requires no internet connection.
   - D) It is limited to storing system backups only.
2. Which device is NOT typically used for local storage backups?
   - A) Flash drive
   - B) External hard drive
   - C) SD card
   - D) Smartphone
3. What type of backup is essential to restore an operating system and installed applications?
   - A) File backup
   - B) Cloud backup
   - C) System backup
   - D) Hardware backup
4. Which of the following is a disadvantage of local storage?
   - A) Easy access from anywhere
   - B) Vulnerability to physical damage
   - C) Requires internet connection
   - D) Limited storage capacity
5. Which storage option generally provides the fastest data retrieval?
   - A) Cloud storage

- B) External hard drive
- C) Flash drive
- D) SD card

Open Ended Questions: Answer the following questions in complete sentences:

1. Explain the difference between file backups and system backups.
2. Describe a scenario where cloud storage would be more beneficial than local storage.
3. Why is it important to have a backup strategy in place?

Answer Key:

Fill in the Blank:

1. A **file** backup involves saving copies of individual files.
2. A **system** backup creates a snapshot of the entire system.
3. **Cloud** storage allows data to be accessed via the internet.
4. A **flash** drive is a portable storage device used for local backups.
5. **Hardware** failures can result in data loss if there are no backups.

Multiple Choice Questions:

1. B) It offers protection against local hardware failures.
2. D) Smartphone
3. C) System backup
4. B) Vulnerability to physical damage
5. C) Flash drive

Open Ended Questions:

1. File backups involve saving copies of individual files, allowing for easy restoration of specific documents. System backups create a complete image of the system, including the operating system and applications, which is essential for restoring the entire system to its previous state.
2. Cloud storage would be more beneficial than local storage in a scenario where a person frequently travels and needs to access their data from multiple locations. It also provides added security against data loss due to local hardware failures or natural disasters.
3. It is important to have a backup strategy in place to ensure that data can be recovered in case of accidental deletion, hardware failure, or cyber-attacks. Having backups minimizes downtime and prevents data loss, which can be costly and disruptive.

CompTIA Fundamentals FC0-U71 Exam Preparation:

Domain 6 – Security

6.1 – Understanding Fundamental Security Concepts

In today's digital world, understanding fundamental security concepts is crucial. These concepts include confidentiality, integrity, and availability, which are the core principles of information security. Privacy involves protecting personal data on platforms like social networking sites, email, file sharing, and instant messaging. It's important to be aware of personally identifiable information (PII) and government regulations like GDPR. Authentication, authorization, accounting, and non-repudiation are key concepts in ensuring secure access to information and systems.

Fill in the Blank: Fill in the blank with the correct words.

1. The three core principles of information security are confidentiality, integrity, and _.
2. _ refers to the protection of personal data on social networking sites.
3. _ is a regulation that protects personal data and privacy in the European Union.
4. _ authentication requires only one type of identity verification.
5. The least privilege model ensures users have only the _ necessary to perform their tasks.

Word bank: availability, privacy, GDPR, single factor, permissions

Multiple Choice Questions: Choose the correct answer from the choices for each question.

1. Which of the following refers to verifying the identity of a user?
   - A) Authorization
   - B) Authentication
   - C) Accounting
   - D) Non-repudiation
2. What does GDPR stand for?
   - A) General Data Protection Regulation
   - B) Government Data Privacy Regulation
   - C) Global Data Privacy Rights
   - D) General Digital Privacy Rule
3. Which type of account usually has more permissions and control over a system?
   - A) User account
   - B) Guest account
   - C) Administrator account
   - D) Public account
4. What is the purpose of accounting in information security?
   - A) To verify user identities
   - B) To track user activities and access
   - C) To prevent unauthorized access
   - D) To manage user permissions
5. What is the benefit of using multifactor authentication?
   - A) It requires fewer steps to log in
   - B) It provides additional security by requiring multiple forms of verification
   - C) It is faster than single-factor authentication
   - D) It allows for anonymous access

Open Ended Questions: Answer the following questions in complete sentences:

1. Explain the importance of confidentiality in information security.

_____

_____

2. How does the least privilege model enhance security in an organization?

_____

_____

3. Describe a scenario where multifactor authentication would be beneficial.

_____

_____

Answer Key:

Fill in the Blank:

1. availability
2. privacy
3. GDPR
4. single factor
5. permissions

Multiple Choice Questions:

1. B) Authentication
2. A) General Data Protection Regulation
3. C) Administrator account
4. B) To track user activities and access
5. B) It provides additional security by requiring multiple forms of verification

Open Ended Questions:

1. Confidentiality is important in information security because it ensures that sensitive information is only accessible to authorized individuals, preventing unauthorized access and potential data breaches.
2. The least privilege model enhances security by ensuring that users have only the permissions necessary to perform their tasks, reducing the risk of accidental or malicious misuse of systems.
3. Multifactor authentication would be beneficial in a scenario where sensitive data is accessed remotely, such as a company employee accessing company databases from home. This ensures that even if a password is compromised, additional verification is needed to access the data.

6.2 – Device Security and Best Practices

Understanding how to secure devices and implement security best practices is crucial in today's digital world. This worksheet will help you learn about security awareness, securing devices, best practices for device use, and safe browsing practices.

Fill in the Blank: Fill in the blank with the correct words.

1. Social engineering tactics such as _ are used to trick individuals into revealing sensitive information.
2. Installing _ software can help protect your device from viruses and other malicious threats.
3. Keeping your software up-to-date by regularly _ is a key security practice.
4. _ locks can physically secure a device to prevent theft.
5. When downloading software, always ensure it comes from a _ source.

Word bank: patching, phishing, anti-malware, cable, legitimate

---

Multiple Choice Questions: Choose the correct answer from the choices for each question.

1. What is a common method used to authenticate a user on a device?
   - A) Firewall
   - B) Password
   - C) Anti-virus
   - D) Patching
2. Which type of website should you trust for downloading software?
   - A) Random blogs
   - B) OEM websites
   - C) Unofficial forums
   - D) Pop-up ads
3. What does a firewall help protect against?
   - A) Physical theft
   - B) Unauthorized network access
   - C) Software updates
   - D) License expiration
4. What is the primary purpose of a product key?
   - A) To personalize software
   - B) To activate software legally
   - C) To speed up software
   - D) To extend software use
5. Which of the following is a sign of a secure website?
   - A) A broken lock icon
   - B) An invalid certificate
   - C) A valid certificate

- D) A warning message

Open Ended Questions: Answer the following questions in complete sentences:

1. Explain why it is important to remove unnecessary or unwanted software from your device.
2. Describe the difference between open-source and proprietary software licensing.
3. What steps can you take to ensure your online activities remain private on social networking sites?

Answer Key:

Fill in the Blank:

1. Phishing
2. Anti-malware
3. Patching
4. Cable
5. Legitimate

Multiple Choice Questions:

1. B) Password
2. B) OEM websites
3. B) Unauthorized network access
4. B) To activate software legally
5. C) A valid certificate

Open Ended Questions:

1. Removing unnecessary or unwanted software is important because it can free up system resources, improve device performance, and reduce security risks by minimizing potential vulnerabilities.
2. Open-source software licensing allows users to view, modify, and distribute the source code, often for free. Proprietary software licensing restricts access to the source code and typically requires the purchase of a license for use.
3. To ensure privacy on social networking sites, you can adjust privacy settings, limit personal information shared, use strong passwords, and be cautious about the links and apps you interact with.

6.3 – Password Best Practices

In today's digital age, maintaining strong and secure passwords is essential to protect personal and sensitive information. Understanding how to create and manage passwords can help prevent unauthorized access and potential security breaches. This worksheet will help you explore password best practices, including password length, complexity, history, expiration, reuse, and the use of password managers.

Fill in the Blank: Fill in the blank with the correct words.

1. A strong password should have a minimum length of _ characters.
2. Passwords should include a mix of letters, numbers, and _ to enhance complexity.
3. You should avoid _ the same password across multiple sites.
4. It's important to regularly _ your password to maintain security.
5. Password _ can help you manage and store complex passwords safely.

Word bank: expiration, symbols, managers, reuse, change, 12

Multiple Choice Questions: Choose the correct answer from the choices for each question.

1. What is the recommended minimum length for a strong password?
   - A) 6 characters
   - B) 8 characters
   - C) 12 characters
   - D) 16 characters
2. Which of the following does NOT contribute to password complexity?
   - A) Numbers
   - B) Lowercase letters
   - C) Symbols
   - D) Spaces
3. How often should you change your password to enhance security?
   - A) Every week
   - B) Every month
   - C) Every six months
   - D) Every year
4. What is the primary purpose of a password manager?
   - A) To generate weak passwords
   - B) To store and manage passwords securely
   - C) To delete old passwords automatically
   - D) To share passwords with friends
5. Why is it important to change default usernames and passwords on new devices?
   - A) To make them easier to remember
   - B) To prevent unauthorized access
   - C) To avoid forgetting them
   - D) To save storage space

Open Ended Questions: Answer the following questions in complete sentences:

1. Explain why using the same password across multiple sites can be a security risk.

_____

2. Describe the process you would follow if you forgot your password and needed to reset it.

_____

3. Discuss the advantages of using a password manager for storing your passwords.

_____

Answer Key:

Fill in the Blank:

1. 12
2. symbols
3. reuse
4. change
5. managers

Multiple Choice Questions:

1. C) 12 characters
2. D) Spaces
3. C) Every six months
4. B) To store and manage passwords securely
5. B) To prevent unauthorized access

Open Ended Questions:

1. Using the same password across multiple sites is a security risk because if one site is compromised and your password is stolen, hackers can access your accounts on other sites where you used the same password.
2. If I forgot my password, I would go to the login page and click on the "Forgot Password" link. I would then follow the instructions to receive a password reset link via my registered email or a code via text message. After receiving the link or code, I would create a new password.
3. A password manager is advantageous because it can store complex passwords securely, allowing you to use strong, unique passwords for different accounts without having to remember each one. It also helps in automatically filling in login details, saving time and reducing the risk of entering incorrect passwords.

6.4 – Encryption Use Cases

Encryption is a key concept in securing digital data. It involves converting plain text into cipher text to protect it from unauthorized access. There are two main types of data encryption: data at rest and data in transit. Data at rest refers to data stored on a device, while data in transit is data being transmitted over a network.

Fill in the Blank: Fill in the blank with the correct words.

1. Data that is stored on a device and not being transmitted is called "data at _."
2. The process of converting plain text into unreadable text is known as _.
3. _ text is readable by humans, whereas cipher text is not.
4. Encrypting data sent over email is an example of securing data _.
5. A _ is used to encrypt data on mobile devices to prevent unauthorized access.

Word bank: cipher, rest, encryption, plain, in transit

Multiple Choice Questions: Choose the correct answer from the choices for each question.

1. What is the main purpose of encryption?
   - A) Increase internet speed
   - B) Protect data from unauthorized access
   - C) Improve computer graphics
   - D) Reduce storage space
2. Which of the following is an example of data in transit?
   - A) A file stored on a USB drive
   - B) An email being sent
   - C) A photo saved on a smartphone
   - D) A document on a desktop
3. What type of encryption is used to secure websites?
   - A) VPN
   - B) HTTPS
   - C) FTP
   - D) SMTP
4. Which device is most likely to use disk-level encryption?
   - A) Desktop computer
   - B) Smartwatch
   - C) Router
   - D) Printer
5. Which method is typically used to encrypt data on mobile applications?
   - A) Firewall
   - B) VPN
   - C) Disk encryption
   - D) Application-level encryption

Open Ended Questions: Answer the following questions in complete sentences:

1. Describe the difference between plain text and cipher text.

2. Explain why it is important to encrypt data at rest on a mobile device.

3. How does a VPN help in encrypting data in transit?

Answer Key:

Fill in the Blank:

1. **rest**
2. **encryption**
3. **plain**
4. **in transit**
5. **cipher**

Multiple Choice Questions:

1. B) Protect data from unauthorized access
2. B) An email being sent
3. B) HTTPS
4. A) Desktop computer
5. D) Application-level encryption

Open Ended Questions:

1. Plain text is readable by humans and can be easily understood, whereas cipher text is scrambled and unreadable without the proper decryption key.
2. Encrypting data at rest on a mobile device is important to protect sensitive information from being accessed by unauthorized users if the device is lost or stolen.
3. A VPN helps encrypt data in transit by creating a secure tunnel between the user's device and the internet, ensuring that data sent and received is protected from eavesdropping.

6.5 - Wireless Network Security

Wireless networks, like the ones we use at home or school, need to be secure to protect our data and privacy. This worksheet will help you understand how to configure security settings for a small wireless network. We'll look at important concepts such as changing the network name, setting passwords, and understanding different types of encryption.

Fill in the Blank: Fill in the blank with the correct words.

1. The network name of a wireless network is also known as the __.
2. It is important to change the default __ to secure your wireless network.
3. __ is used to protect data as it travels over wireless networks.
4. __ is a type of encryption that is stronger than WPA.
5. __ networks do not require a password and are less secure.

Word bank: WPA2, SSID, Unencrypted, Password, Encryption

Multiple Choice Questions: Choose the correct answer from the choices for each question.

1. What is the main purpose of changing the SSID of a wireless network?
   - A) To increase the speed of the network
   - B) To make the network more secure
   - C) To connect more devices
   - D) To reduce interference
2. Which of the following is the strongest type of wireless encryption?
   - A) Open
   - B) WPA
   - C) WPA2
   - D) WPA3
3. What is a pre-shared key used for in wireless networks?
   - A) Identifying devices
   - B) Sharing files
   - C) Encrypting data
   - D) Increasing signal strength
4. Why should the default password of a wireless network be changed?
   - A) To make it easier to remember
   - B) To improve network coverage
   - C) To prevent unauthorized access
   - D) To save energy
5. Which of the following is a drawback of using an unencrypted network?
   - A) Faster connection speed
   - B) Easier access for guests
   - C) Increased security risks
   - D) Better signal quality

Open Ended Questions: Answer the following questions in complete sentences:

1. Why is it important to use encryption on a wireless network?
2. How does changing the SSID help in securing a wireless network?
3. Describe a situation where you might prefer using WPA3 over WPA2.

Answer Key:

Fill in the Blank:

1. SSID
2. Password
3. Encryption
4. WPA2
5. Unencrypted

Multiple Choice Questions:

1. B) To make the network more secure
2. D) WPA3
3. C) Encrypting data
4. C) To prevent unauthorized access
5. C) Increased security risks

Open Ended Questions:

1. It is important to use encryption on a wireless network to protect sensitive information from being accessed by unauthorized users.
2. Changing the SSID helps in securing a wireless network by making it less obvious to others, especially if the default SSID is used by many.
3. You might prefer using WPA3 over WPA2 when you need the highest level of security, such as in a business environment with sensitive data.